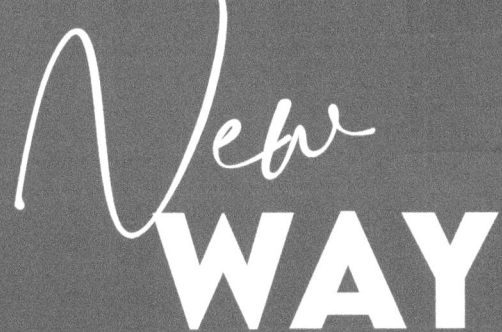

New WAY

SHELTERED THROUGH THE STORM

New Way

SHELTERED THROUGH THE STORM
Copyright © 2022 Magda Joseph

All scripture references used in this book were taken from the Holy Bible, Common English Version and can be found at http://thebiblegateway.com.

Editor: Crystal S. Wright

ISBN: 979-8-9860947-1-7

10 9 8 7 6 5 4 3 2 1
Printed in the United States

Priceless Publishing®
pricelesspublishing.co
Lauderhill, Florida

Contents

Sheltered

Acknowledgments

I give thanks to God, first and foremost.
Without the love of God, I wouldn't be alive today.
His grace has saved me endlessly, and for that I am forever grateful.

Secondly, I express deep and sincere gratitude to my beautiful mother, for being there for me even when I thought she wasn't. No one can replace you in my heart, Mom.

Thank you to my sister Johnna, for always having the right jokes at the wrong time. I appreciate that you never judged me — even through my darkest days. You kept loving me and my children, who you cared for like they are her own.

To my Aunt Arnee: You deserve the most gratitude and appreciation for your never-ending prayers and words of encouragement. You exude the love of God everyday by just existing and being who you are.

Thank you to my lifetime partner Jarvis, for always being there. Thank you for loving me even on the days I made it hard for you to. I love you and am excited to continue life with you.

Big thank you to Dr. Sidjae Price for believing in me, and being a true servant of God. Dr. Price, you saw something in me that I had not envisioned in a million years.

Thank you so much for making a dream I didn't even know I had, come true.

To Crystal Wright: thank you for your patience with me through the editing process.

Lastly, I want to congratulate myself for sticking to the process and doing the hard self-work necessary to get my story out and onto these pages.

To God be the glory!

Chapter 1: Remembering When

For most people, it is a struggle to recall a memory before the age of 5. That is not the case for me. My earliest memory is of myself at the tender age of 2 or 3, standing in my crib and watching my parents argue. I remember the layout of the room, including where the dressers were placed and the picture frames were nailed. Holding onto the bars of the crib, I observed them knocking things over, yelling and crying. I even remember that my mother slapped my father as they continued the verbal abuse on one another.

Despite all this, the most distinct detail from that memory was the thought that the two people that loved me so much, couldn't love each other. That is the only memory I can recall of my parents arguing. I'm pretty sure I blocked the rest of the memories of such moments. My parents split when I was about 4 years old. I truly believe that they loved each other but just weren't on the same page when it came to life choices and relationship expectations.

After my parents split up, communication with my biological father was irregular, but I always looked forward to our time together. Spending time with him was always fun. Getting to see my relatives on his side of the family, going to church, and just being around good company made me feel loved. Whenever I would ask my mom about my dad, she always brushed me off or caught an attitude. *"Why are you worried about him? Is he here right now?"* was her favorite line. So, I learned to not ask about him.

Soon, a man named James entered our life when I was 4. He was kind and caring but within a year, he was no longer in the picture. Between the ages of 5 and 7, my Mom and James separated and she dated Morris, who abused her physically. I can remember my mom getting punched in the face by Morris, because she went out without telling him. Or because he just had a bad day and decided to let his anger out on her. Numerous nights I would hear my mother's scream, and I would sneakily take the house phone and call 911, hanging up after whispering my home address to the operator. Morris just was not a very nice guy. He let his anger get the best of him.

One morning my mother bravely changed all the locks to the house. She picked me up from school, dropped me off at home and went back to work around 3:15pm. I was 7 years old at this time, and pretty self-sufficient. There was always food prepared for me and Mom's one rule was that I should never answer the door in her absence, even if I knew who it was. So, unless she had told me to expect someone, I would not even look through a window if there was a knock on the door.

That same evening at around 5pm, Morris came to the house. I knew it was him because his car made a distinct clicking noise and squeaked from what I often heard the adults call, "a bad timing belt." I rarely kept lights on, so I just turned the tv down and I could hear him calling my mother's name in the window.

He walked around the house checking all the doors, becoming more frustrated as he realized his key did not work.

I grabbed the house phone, ran into the closet and called my Mom's job, saying there was an emergency. I told Mom that Morris was outside checking all the doors and yelling our names, but that I didn't answer. My mom told me to, *"Stay quiet and DO NOT OPEN THE DOOR."* I did exactly as I was told. I stayed on the phone with her until he got back in his car and left, after piling the trash bags full of belongings in his car.

By the age of 8 James was present again, and that was a breath of fresh air. He is still my stepfather today, and is the sweetest guy ever. I have never heard him raise his voice at my mom, call her out of her name or escalate to arguing with her even when she was difficult to get along with. It's like he knew all the right things to say — or not say, and for that, I always admired him as a man even as a young child. My appreciation for him only grew stronger as I matured. My mother needed someone like him in her life, and so did I.

But, I wished that I could see my dad more often. I remember times when my dad would come to our house to see me or pick me up and somehow an argument would always arise. My stepdad rarely intervened, and whenever he did it was to de-escalate the situation. Over time, seeing my parents argue became the norm for me. The more they argued, the less I saw my dad. Yes, I had a father figure in James, but I still wanted my dad.

From an early age, the relationship between my mother and I was a typical mother-daughter, loving one. I would watch her get dressed and put on her make-up. I would pass her the brush as she showed me how to put her hair in a ponytail. I would pick out cute tops and purses for her when we went shopping. The best part about our relationship was being in the kitchen with her while she cooked and taught me the importance of being able to make a meal from start to finish, whether for myself or my future husband.

Even though she had a man by her side, I watched my mom work hard to provide. For as long as I can remember, my mom has worked 9am - 11pm Tuesdays through Sundays as a cook in a Chinese restaurant. She worked on every holiday and birthday that fell within that schedule. My stepdad was always traveling between Haiti and Panama for his business, so he wasn't home often either. Because of this, I spent my evenings home alone after school, or with my cousins who lived in our neighborhood.

I enjoyed seeing my cousins Urma, Elouinia and Berline. Though their mother and my uncle had split up, our mothers remained really good friends. Their mother was like an aunt to me. A lot of the childhood memories that molded me in my younger years involved these 3 cousins, but the day their uncle Ed came to Florida from Haiti was one of the worst days in my life. I went from enjoying the time spent at my cousin's house to begging my mom to not let me stay another night.

I wasn't brave enough to tell her why I didn't want to stay. I didn't know at the age of 7 how to articulate to my mom that I was being touched in my sleep by Ed. See I was always the type to wake up in the middle of the night and just stare at the wall and think deep thoughts. Like, *how do the stars stay up in the sky? Who is God, really? Why is a dog called a dog?*

On one particular night I was up thinking my deep thoughts when Ed entered the room, believing that I was asleep. My aunt lived in a two-bedroom apartment in Sistrunk, Florida. She had her room and my cousins had theirs. But when uncle came into town, he shared a room with my cousins. Looking back, I have no clue how it made sense to my aunt to have her brother sleep in her daughters' room instead of on the couch.

At first, I thought he was getting up to use the restroom, but he walked to the door, opened it and paused. I guess he was checking his surroundings to make sure everyone was asleep. My cousins and I were sleeping on the floor pallets that were made with thick covers like it was a big sleepover.

The room was dark — the only light you could see was the streetlight peeking through the window and furniture casting a Z shadow on the wall. Ed walked over to me and touched my leg before pausing, as if he was trying to see if I would respond. But I didn't move. That's when he, wearing only his boxers, kneeled down next to me, and started caressing from my legs up to my thighs.

Immediately, the thoughts in my head shifted from the color of the sky to, *Is this really happening to me? What is happening right now? Why did he choose me? Did he already touch my cousins?* So many thoughts rushed through my mind at once. Before I knew it, his member was out of his boxers and on my body. Not sure what my next move should be, I shifted slowly as if I were moving in my sleep to cover myself. He backed up slowly in the dark, as if he was putting a baby to sleep and didn't want to wake them up. After shifting positions, he tried to continue but I seized the opportunity to move.

I got up and rushed to the bathroom. I just sat in there, crying and confused. My head was filled with thoughts as I tried to process what had just happened to me. *Why is this happening? Is this something planned? Did I say or do something to make him think it was okay to touch me? Do my cousins know he came to my room? Are they awake? Did he touch them first?*

I don't recall how long I stayed in that bathroom, crying and thinking, thinking and crying. I remember telling my aunt after coming out of the bathroom that I wanted to go home and her response was that I should go back to sleep. In the morning I was just distant, regretting being at that house and still reeling from the ordeal.

There were about two more nights like that with Ed. I didn't know what to do. *Should I say something or just let it go?* I was too scared so I kept it to myself, but told my mom I would rather stay home than spend evenings over there. Of course, she still brought me over there but I don't blame her — she didn't know what was going on. I always made sure to go home with her and not spend the night.

A couple of months passed. One of my cousins told her mom that Ed had touched her. As I feared, her mother didn't believe her or take her side. No one spoke of it ever again. That reinforced my fear that I would not be believed, so I chose to not speak up.

Chapter 2: No Trust In Courage

When I turned 9 years old, my mother got pregnant with my sister. For so long it was just us two, and now I was about to have a sibling! That was exciting for me and the family. My sister Johnna was the company I would keep around the house. *I wouldn't have to feel alone anymore!* Or so I thought. Little did I know that due to Mom's work schedule, I would be the one to raise my sister. As time went on, mom usually had aunts or older cousins come in from Haiti to live with us until they got on their feet. Sometimes she even rented out a room to get some extra income.

On one of my stepfather's trips to Haiti, he returned with his dad. It was pretty cool to meet and spend time with another member of the family and hear stories about Haiti. But that joy was short-lived as my step-grandfather became the second man to molest me. The worst part about it, was that this time I couldn't run away because he lived in my home. For two years prior, I had mentally tortured myself for not speaking up about my 'Uncle' Ed molesting me, and here was an entirely new person breaking me into even smaller pieces.

When around my mother and stepdad, we were like a regular family. When my parents weren't in sight, my step-grandfather behaved completely differently. It started off with him giving me hugs that were too tight and lasted too long. Then at age 10, he started watching me while I took showers. Imagine being a young girl, barely understanding the pre-pubescent changes taking place in your body, taking a shower while a grown man watches you with a grin.

It was clear that he took pleasure in watching me in spite of my discomfort. You're probably wondering why I didn't lock the doors. Well, sometimes there were no doorknobs on our doors, to keep my sister from locking herself in rooms. Also, it is easy to pick a lock. Day after day, for about 2 years, if he wasn't visiting Haiti, my step-grandfather was at home with me. It became his regular routine to watch me while I showered, sometimes pleasuring himself as he did so. I made sure that he didn't look at or touch my sister — who was only two at this time — but I couldn't seem to protect myself.

I remember sitting in my middle school class wondering how many other students were silently suffering like me. *Was this something to be considered normal?* It can't be normal, I concluded, *because deep down inside it just doesn't feel right.* There were times when I wanted to just stand up in class and scream, in hopes that someone would understand. But I managed to hide behind my good grades which never slipped. No one could see that something was wrong — but everything was wrong. Over time, I went from knowing that something was wrong, to almost feeling like I deserved to be molested.

No one is coming to save me, I thought dejectedly, *I can't even save myself.*

There were so many times when I sat alone in my bedroom, practicing how I would tell my mom about what was happening to me. But then I would think about my cousin who told her mom, and was accused of lying. It wasn't just her mother either. No one believed her. I overheard the conversation between adults about what my cousin confessed to. They made it seem like she imagined or dreamed being molested that night.

Would everyone think I was lying too, or would they believe me and save me? So many people were around me every day smiling, laughing and being happy but no one could see that I was walking around with a secret that was burdening me at the age of 11. I kept silent, and told myself to just be quiet for another hour...another day...another week. But my step-grandfather got bolder and bolder as time went on.

One night after watching me shower, he barged into my room while I was getting dressed and stood staring at me. A few long minutes afterwards, I heard Mom arrive home and drop her keys on the kitchen table. Hearing her too, he hurried into his room which was adjacent to mine, and shut his door. I had never before seen that look of fear on his face, worried that he had almost been caught. For the first time I witnessed the person who made me afraid, feeling afraid. Still reeling from his presence in my room, I thought nothing of it.

Within the next minute Mom came into my room to greet me and let me know that she was home. A part of me — the optimistic part — thought she knew what my step-grandfather was doing to me, but another part of me — the heartbroken part — knew she didn't know. He had run into his room too quickly for her to have seen him. Even as I made the choice to remain silent, I was disappointed in myself, that I was wasting such a perfect opportunity. My mother was my closest friend and I couldn't bring myself to tell her that I was hurting at the hands of trusted men in my life.

Later that night, he entered my room while everyone was asleep. I was awake, still thinking about how I missed an opportunity to pour out my broken heart to Mom, when I heard his door squeak open. My door was pushed open some seconds after. As he opened my room door, and entered, the moonlight coming into the window illuminated his shadow and confirmed my worst fear — he was back. My heart began to race. Prior to that night he had only watched from the door while I dressed, but he had clearly become more confident in his actions. He walked over to my bed and climbed in.

I could smell his breath as he got closer to me. He had already undressed, as if he had been waiting for everyone to go to bed so he could make his move. I was wearing a night gown with buttons, which he took his time to undo. I felt the cold, unending circle of metal on my skin, as he placed a ring on my finger, like he was marking me as his. I felt confused, angry and scared all at once. *Did he think a ring gave him permission to violate me?!*

He bundled my open nightgown to the side and climbed on top of me, pressing his large body against mine and forcing his member into my virgin body. My body froze. Maybe there is truth to the expression of being 'paralyzed with fear'. I distinctly remember the profound helplessness I felt as I lay there with tears in my eyes. I had never felt as alone as I did in that moment. He finished and ejaculated between my legs, then walked out of my room with a sense of pride.

Hands trembling, I gingerly got up as soon as I heard him shut his door. I made my way into the bathroom, with my heart beating and mind racing. As I sat in the tub rinsing my body of the guilt, hurt, pain and disgust I was feeling, I heard Mom's voice and blow dryer through the walls. I guess she had washed her hair and was having a casual conversation with my stepdad. I guess everyone wasn't asleep as I had thought. I guess she didn't hear me in the bathroom over her conversation and hair drying.

I got up out of the tub, wrapped myself in a towel and walked to her bedroom door. I stood there, for what felt like hours, trying to build up the courage to tell her what was done to me. I raised my little fist up over and over and over, imagining myself knocking on Mom's door. But I didn't do it. I eventually walked back into my bedroom and shut the door. My whole body was shaking, as I paced back and forth for I-don't-know-how-long.

Then out of nowhere, it's like something took over and Courage came. I walked to my door, opened it, and walked straight to my mother's door and knocked confidently. I knocked harder and harder until she answered. She opened her door and looked at me and I looked back at her, but the words I needed wouldn't come out.

My step-grandfather's room was between mine and my mom's. At that moment I heard Him open his door and as courage took over again, I pushed myself into my Mom's room and away from him. Holding out my hand, I showed her the ring on my finger and released the words, *"Grandpa raped me."*

The sound that came out of my mother's mouth was indescribable. It was like the wailing scream of a mother who had lost her only child. Her knees gave out and she fell to the floor screaming. It was like she suddenly was feeling every ounce of my pain. My stepdad did not hear what I said to her, so he just stood there befuddled, trying to figure out what was going on. But I couldn't bring myself to repeat the words, and Mom wouldn't stop screaming and crying like a mad woman at a funeral. I could tell that He was still standing at his doorway, pretending like he didn't know what had just happened.

My mother finally calmed herself down enough to stand up and tell James what I had said about his father. As she repeated my words out loud to him, she fell to the ground again in despair. My stepdad sank to the ground, held his head in his hands and cried. After some time, Mom picked herself up off the floor and screamed at Him to get out of her house, telling Him that he was no longer welcome. My stepdad couldn't do anything but sit on the floor. I could tell he felt disappointment and shame for the actions of his father.

How could someone so sweet and loving have come from such a monster, I wondered.

My stepdad eventually got up off the floor and walked out the room to his father. Before I could see what happened next, Mom slammed her bedroom door shut, locking me inside with her. For a while she just looked at me, not saying a word, while tears ran down her face. It was almost as if she had experienced the same violation that I had, but didn't want to admit it. I could tell by the look on her face that she was sorry that she had not saved me sooner. I again showed her the ring that He had given to me. She asked me what happened and I told her exactly. She reassured me that he was gone, and wouldn't be back in the house ever again.

To my dismay, my mother then told me to not tell anyone or talk about what happened that night. She asked me what happened and I repeated my words detailing the truth, and she responded with, *"I just told you not to tell anybody or talk about what happened tonight. If the police come to the house or if someone asks you something, do not say anything."* She asked me one more time what happened and by that time, I understood the assignment.

I could not believe it. I had finally summoned enough courage to speak of my pain and confide in my best friend, and was now being told to keep it to myself. *How was keeping this ordeal to myself protecting me?* I had already done that for so long, and it didn't help one bit! I stayed quiet and it still hurt. *Was she protecting him?* But at that age in a Haitian home, children did not have a voice. I kept quiet. I didn't even bother telling her of the years my step-grandfather watched me shower, or bringing up Ed.

That exchange broke me more than the theft of my virginity itself, and the festered wound of years of abuse. It's bad enough that I was molested by someone who I trusted, but to be instructed by my mom to keep quiet about it was more painful that I could have imagined. In my eyes, there was no reward for my bravery in turning to her. *What was the point?* There was no balm or outlet for my pain. At the age of 11 I learned that my problems are just that — my problems. From that point on I didn't care to share anything positive. I lost trust in everyone.

Although the monster was no longer physically in the house, his presence still lingered. I felt unsafe and lost trust in my mother. I realized that if something bad happened to me again, I was expected to be quiet about it. If something bothered me or made me uncomfortable, I had to reassure myself, *Magda, don't even bother because nothing will be done about it. Just keep it to yourself. Solve your own problems.* Keeping quiet was just my family's traditional solution to problem solving. They chose to pretend like It never happened.

I never saw Him again — not at any family gatherings, or even just randomly around the neighborhood. I don't know where He ended up that night or afterwards. He was just (physically) gone. In the Haitian culture it's embarrassing to admit to something like being molested. So, for years afterwards that's what I adhered to, and over time I almost forgot that it had ever happened. But subconsciously I was hurting from an untended, infected wound, coping as best I could with the secret pain.

But I remembered something my dad always told me, *"God loves you and is always listening to you. Just remember to pray."*

Chapter 3: The Rebel Within

Life as I knew it changed with that encounter, and seemed confusing and unreal. I always stayed in my room, not talking much to anybody unless I was spoken to first. When I got home from school each evening, I ate and went straight to my room. I didn't come out unless I was needed, or I had to use the bathroom. I watched television day in and day out. I lost my love for reading, and was just in my own little world — or the fictional world of the actors — everyday.

My Mom worked long hours so I barely saw her anyway. And when she did come home I usually pretended to already be in bed to avoid interactions with her. To be honest, I don't even think my mother noticed the drastic changes in me. Or if she noticed, maybe she just chalked it up to normal adolescent changes. I was always a quiet child anyway, but this time my silence was loud and I almost drowned in it.

I was introduced to the Chatline by one of my cousins. The Chatline was basically a platform to chat on the phone with other people in your city. The main rule was that participants had to be 18 and over to chat, but I was in middle school having conversations with grown men over the phone. Don't judge me. It's not my fault there wasn't an age check. It was an automated service that answered and you just press numbers until you get to the desired chatroom. I initially sat quietly and listened to how others in the individual conference rooms chatted with each other. I paid keen attention to the lingo the older women used until I gathered the confidence to start a chat with someone.

On the Chatline I could be whomever I wanted, whenever I wanted. I spent hours on the Chatline to escape from the real world. The Chatline was a place where my voice could be heard and was welcome. I didn't have to show my face or worry about seeing anyone if I didn't want to. Surprisingly, I did come across several people who were cool and actually kept in touch.

Further along in our friendship, many admitted to lying about their age as well. Like me, they just wanted a chance to escape from the reality of their lives and be whoever they chose to be. I didn't know it then but I was trauma bonding. Not too long afterwards the Chatline was shut down. I made it through middle school with A's and B's and left that world behind me — it was time for high school.

We all get to a place in life where we feel like we are supposed to fit in, and we end up comparing ourselves to others. High school was that time for me, but I decided that I didn't want to 'fit in'. In order to fit in you have to do what others did, talk like others talked and dressed like others dressed. I was always the quiet smart girl in elementary school and in middle school. High school would be no different if it was up to me. I just wanted to get through it and get on with my life.

My high school life was not the typical one. I didn't play any sports and only joined the French club to get extra credits for school. While I did socialize enough to make friends, they were only my friends on the school compound. No one came to my house to do homework or study. If I was invited to their house, I just said my mom would not allow me, or that I had to babysit my little sister. I made it through high school with some good grades and walked across the graduation stage with a smile on my face.

As I got older I noticed that my dad made an appearance more often. I loved it because that meant I got a chance to see my paternal relatives. I remember when visiting his parents, they always asked me if I remembered who they were, because I was the grandchild that was rarely around. But I knew who they were and I loved the close bond that they had. Of all the times my father came to pick me up, I never mustered up the courage to tell him what had happened to me during his absence.

All I could hear in my head was Mom's firm voice telling me to keep quiet. Besides, what if he already knew and was keeping quiet about it too? *Was my dad that type of person?* It was hard to tell when so many years had slipped away without me getting to know him well. I knew he loved me and cared for me, but I simply did not know him. He did not know me either, no matter how many times he said he did. He didn't.

Growing up as a girl in Haitian culture was tough. My life was built around school, home and church. There was no opportunity for friends and certainly not boyfriends. So, I was school-smart, but not very street-smart. I was so sheltered growing up, that as soon as I turned 18 I was ready to explore the world outside the four walls of my mother's house. The rebel in me came out! The first man who I chose willingly to have sex with was someone I thought I loved.

But after the encounter he basically discarded me. All that did was make me transform into a monster, because if men were nothing before, they certainly became dirt pits in my eyes after that.

I didn't go away to college like many high schoolers who I knew. I attended a community college majoring in Elementary Education with a minor in Psychology, and the relationship with my mom grew worse. She wanted me to study to become a nurse or doctor, but that's just not what I wanted to do. In the Haitian community, you would think becoming a nurse is the only occupation that there is. Honestly, I wasn't even sure about what I really wanted to do. I just knew those careers were not it. I knew though that whatever I did, I wanted to help people.

There were many days during community college that I stayed out for 3 days at a time, sometimes even a week. I didn't call my mom to let her know my whereabouts. She would try to contact me though. Some days I would answer and some days I didn't want to explain myself or argue so I didn't answer. It was easier for me to spend my days out instead of going home to deal with the frequent arguments with Mom. Eventually, I felt like school was getting in the way of my fun, so I stopped going.

My priorities were definitely not in order. I worked and blew my money on partying, shopping and supporting my soft habit of smoking marijuana. Mom always asked me what I was doing with my money in my free time and I always told her to mind her business. In my mind, I didn't think she really cared. I felt like she was just being nosy. All I wanted then was to get attention from others to fill the emptiness that I felt inside. It probably wasn't the best way to cope but it's the way that I knew.

Through

Chapter 4: Love Lives On

Now that I was more mature and my father thought that we were getting closer, he felt compelled to tell me about why he and Mom split when I was young. I had long since concluded that the break-up was my mom's fault anyway so I didn't care about the details. I was just happy for the chance to see my dad again and spend some time with his side of the family.

Although I enjoyed spending time with my dad, I didn't always accept the opportunity, because I felt as though it was forced or insincere. I wanted to be able to say my dad's a part of my life, but I had not truly opened my heart to connect with him. The only thing that was confident I knew of my dad, was that he loved me.

I always heard my aunts, uncles and cousins on his side talk about my grandmother and her mission work in Haiti. My grandma started out by helping the needy children in the neighborhoods in Haiti. Soon schools, churches and an orphanage were built. The work my grandparents were doing in Haiti was the work of God — pure and simple. It was inspiring to see something so small have such a big impact. My grandfather was a well-known Pastor in Haiti. So, I know that I came from a bloodline that is blessed and highly favored. Having those two grandparents as the backbone of our family, gave us a sense of pride and determination.

One day, I received a phone call from my dad saying that Grandpa was sick. I am not sure if it was because of the lack of relationship between my father and I, but I couldn't really tell when he was angry, or sad about the situation. You would have thought Grandpa just had a case of the common cold. *He's an old man,* I thought. *He's always in the hospital. He'll get out and he'll be fine.* But Grandpa being sick was way more crucial than my dad made it seem. I wish Dad had just straight up told me that Grandpa was dying.

My Grandfather passed away in March of 2010. His death was devastating. Although I had experienced the death of a loved one before, I still hadn't really grasped what death was. I had never seen my family like this. I could still see and feel their love for each other, but there was a brokenness. My grandfather was a great man so his passing was a big deal. His funeral was packed from wall to wall — not an empty seat in the building. Some people had to stand — people that loved him, people that he'd ministered to, people that he'd helped.

Everyone who was in attendance was there because my grandfather had changed their life in some way. Grandpa was so well respected that he had a funeral service in Haiti and had a funeral service in the States. But my pain was a little bit different. I didn't know my grandfather the way everybody else did, but I was hurt. I didn't cry in front of everybody, but I cried. I cried because it sucked. We all wrote letters to Grandpa and placed it in his casket with him. If my world wasn't dark enough before then, I think it got a little dimmer after Grandpa passed.

So here I am — four years out of high school. I didn't have a clue who I was, what I wanted do or where I wanted to go. The relationship I had with my mom at the time wasn't the best, and I didn't know where the relationship with my Dad was going. I felt lost. This was a familiar feeling and one I knew so well from a very young age. So I did what I knew best — found ways to feel alive. What way to feel more alive at the age of 20 than to party and drink?

I was never home. Sometimes I'd be gone for weeks at a time, ignoring my mom's phone calls because I didn't want to be bothered. I was never really in the streets hanging with the wrong people. I had reconnected with an old friend from high school named Janide. I was at her house day in and day out. I would go home to shower and change into my work clothes, just to get off work and head straight to the girls'. As far as I was concerned, it was better than being locked up at home getting into petty arguments with Mom about my life choices. When I wasn't with the girls, I was chatting online and meeting new people to fill the void I was feeling.

In September of 2011, I met a married couple named Jarvis and Leah while chatting online. They were interested in my friendship, just as much as I was interested in theirs. I kept this relationship to myself, as I didn't want to be judged, or have my sense of freedom restricted.

Janide and I started hanging out more and going to clubs. We were basically living the college life without being in college. At that point she wasn't just a mere friend — she was my sister.

A night out in the city with the girls was always fun. Nothing else ever mattered when we were out. If there was a party or a fun event happening, we found a way to get on the list and make it a girls' night out. I'm not sure what anyone else said but my goal was to drown out that lonely feeling. But no matter how many drinks I had, or how many blunts I smoked, it didn't make me feel less alone in a room full of people.

This particular night I had to work late. I didn't have a car at the time and Janide had agreed to come and pick me up. When I called her and told her I was ready, she said she was out getting a tattoo. So, I'm sitting outside the mall a little after midnight waiting on my friend to come pick me up and she's getting a tattoo. I felt a wave of disappointment wash over me, and all the disappointments I ever experienced just replayed in my head at once.

From being quieted by my mom, to my ex-boyfriend leaving for college and getting a girl pregnant, to the awful relationship with my parents — it all came flowing down. Something so small to everyone else, was a traumatic response to me. At this point in life I had already learned that you don't wait around and hope life gives you what you want but get things done myself. So I started walking home to Melrose Park from Sawgrass Mall, and the transit bus I need to take me straight home stopped running from the mall at 11pm.

 As I was walking home, Jarvis and Leah so happened to call and ask me what I was up to. Of course, my reply was, *"I am walking home from work. I had a ride but she had more important things to do."*

Without hesitation, they came and picked me up while I was walking down Broward Boulevard headed towards Melrose where my mom's house was. It was the first time I met them and I spent the night at their house. That was the beginning of me having two 'friends with benefits' at one time. It definitely brought excitement to my lonely world. I don't know what I was chasing or hoping for, but all I know is it felt great. An innocent card game of Tonk turned into a night that I wouldn't forget.

In all the time that I spent chatting with the couple and getting to know them, I never sensed that they were having their own problems. I just figured they were into having a third party in their marriage and enjoyed the fun as I did. I loved the fact I had a different set of friends around that didn't judge me or make me feel uncomfortable. After a while, I started noticing that Leah was around less and Jarvis was around more, and I knew something was wrong. When I finally asked, Jarvis was honest with me and told me that they had separated. Leah and I remained friends, but she never wanted to hang out again. She always stayed to herself or whoever she was dating at the time, while Jarvis and I continued our friendship with benefits.

From the outside looking in, most people thought I was the cause of their fallen marriage, not knowing that I was rooting for them all along. *Because, if they split where would that leave me?* I wanted both friendships. But the reality of it all was that Jarvis was fighting for someone who was done fighting for him. I watched my friend fall apart, all while still being there for me whenever needed him.

In time, the friendship that I had with Jarvis meshed with the friendship that I had with Janide. I had two best friends, but one with a little extra fun involved. They both got along, but I found myself wanting to be around Jarvis more. I felt like he understood me. He knew things about me that even Janide did not know. He listened to whatever I wanted to talk about, and I was a listening ear for him as well. Regardless of how much we confided in each other, both of us were fighting demons.

While at work one day, I got a call from my cousin, Loudrige. She told me that everyone was taking a trip to go visit Grandma, as she was getting weaker. That same night there was a big party in the city which I decided to attend instead. I doubted that my job would have given me the time off on such short notice, so I didn't even bother to check. Little did I know, that was my last chance to see my grandmother alive. It tore my heart into a million pieces, to know that I chose to go out and get drunk instead of seeing her.

My grandmother was just as loving as my grandfather. I mean, it took a strong woman to be with my grandfather, and that she was. My grandmother did mission work in Haiti. She was always finding a way to donate food, clothes and money to people in need there. This was in addition to the school, church and orphanage that she helped to build there. The orphanage was called House of HOPE, and built through the La Paix Foundation. Not only did Grandma raise 10 children of her own, but she was saving and helping other families as well. The impact that both my grandparents had made on the lives of others made me proud to be a part of their bloodline. But now they were gone.

Here we go again, I thought. I had not even processed the death of my grandfather, and now my family was planning the funeral of the matriarch of the family. I couldn't blame this disappointment on anyone but myself. I let myself down by not going to see my grandmother when she was alive. Nothing or no one was more important than her that night when I chose to go to the club, but my heartache and hunger for excitement led me to choose otherwise. That was the beginning of a downward spiral for me. Jarvis and I got a hotel room the night before my grandmother's funeral, and that was the first night I popped a molly.

The funeral was phenomenal. We all wore white for our Angel, sang songs that Grandpa wrote and showered our mother with loving memories of her beautiful heart and soul. The family decided to bury our grandparents in the wall at the cemetery, placing Grandma and Grandpa right next to each other. When the pallbearer opened the placement where Grandpa's casket was to place Grandma's, the roses we had thrown on Grandpa's casket 2 years prior were still fresh and blooming. I was shocked. The red, white and yellow roses were as bright and colorful then as when we had placed them there. Even in the afterlife, Grandpa was still honoring Grandma with fresh flowers. I too longed for a deep, unconditional and endless love like that.

Chapter 5: Losing

It was never my intention to start a different drug other than marijuana. I always felt in the safe zone with marijuana. But at the moment, I didn't care. I was ready for a feeling that I couldn't explain. I didn't know what to expect. Taking the molly that night before my grandmother's funeral opened up a door that I didn't want to close. That feeling of being light as a feather was just...great.

I walked outside of the Hometown Suites hotel room in North Lauderdale after taking the molly and stood next to a tree and I swore that the tree gave me special oxygen. I called it my tree of life. I sat under the tree and spoke to God that night, told him my life is in His hands. I told God that I don't know where I'm going from here but I hope He's still there at the end of this mission. I asked Him what was going on. I laughed and cried under that tree.

I was still feeling hurt deep down inside, but physically the molly kept me from sulking in it. The drug made me feel better. I enjoyed the feeling more than anything I had experienced before. Soon, I went from taking mollies to taking ecstasy. Jarvis was the only person who I ever trusted to do drugs with. He never forced me to do anything and he never left me alone when I was high. We were always in it together. Half the time it was my idea, but because I knew he was trying to escape his problems too, it was easy for us to get lost in that world.

As time went on the relationship with my mother and I deteriorated further. At this point, I had already moved out of her house and moved back in numerous times. So, for me to pack my things and move with Jarvis and Janide was nothing special. Jarvis and I moved to get away from living at home with our parents. I believe Janide made the decision to get an apartment with us because she felt like she was losing her friend.

We all moved into a 3 bedroom-2 bath apartment in Lauderhill in May of 2012. That move was short lived, as soon an argument broke out about missing money. I had too much going on in my head to even care about the root of the problem. All I cared about was getting high, drinking and reaping the benefit part of the friendship that I had with Jarvis.

About a month into us moving into the apartment, I found out that I was pregnant. That was certainly not how I had expected or desired for life to work out. *What was I going to do with a baby by a man who was still fighting for his marriage, and fighting his own demons?* I kept the pregnancy to myself and I fell into a deep depression. I didn't even tell the girls. At a time in my life where I was supposed to be happy and celebrate and have a party with my friends and family, I wasn't happy at all.

All I could think about was the number of pills I had taken, and the drunk nights I had while being pregnant. So, I decided not to keep my baby. I was making phone calls to terminate the pregnancy. The only person I told was Jarvis. I could see in his eyes that he didn't want to get rid of the baby. At this time, Jarvis already had 4 boys of his own and Leah was pregnant as well. He understood the circumstances and was there for me regardless.

In August of 2012, I sat on the bus riding to that termination appointment and cried until I caught a headache. I was uneasy about the choice I was about to make. *God placed this gift in your hands and you're just throwing it away,* I thought. It's all I could think. No matter how much I cried out to God for an intervention, my flesh still walked into that clinic and went through with the procedure.

If I was beating myself up before the procedure, you should have seen me afterwards. Oh, I beat myself up about that decision so bad. I pushed everyone away. I felt like a I had failed at life. I felt like I was cruel. I felt like I didn't deserve anything that God had for me. *How could I sit and claim that I love God and then make a choice to throw my baby away?*

I held that guilt inside me for a very long time. But at that time that's the only control I believed I had in my life. Whether it was good or bad, at least I was in control. Little did I know I had lost control. It made me angrier with myself. Once again I found myself locked up in my room, lost. I don't even think Jarvis understood the depths of my emotions during that time. I doubt that he did, because I didn't share my feelings much.

I missed my mom. I was mad at her but it got to the point where I couldn't remember why. I just knew I missed her. Of course, my pride and ego wouldn't let me express that to her. Trying to drown out the feeling of missing her, I would gulp down a drink, or swallow a molly and bask in the euphoric feeling until sunrise. I felt self-hatred. I was angry. I also disappointed in myself. But when I took the drug I didn't have those feelings anymore.

Janide eventually moved out of the apartment and our friendship (in my mind), went out the door with her. To me she was just another person walking away from me. I knew I still wanted my best friend but I let my pride win. *I wasn't going to chase someone who didn't want to stay.* I never considered for a second that maybe she might have been going through her own problems. I was too focused on me to think of anyone else. When the smoke cleared, Jarvis was the only one left on my team. From that point on we were inseparable, although we were still only "friends."

Too lost in our own troubles, we got evicted from our apartment in October of 2012, and Jarvis and I moved into his mom's house. Four months after moving there in February 2013, I found out I was pregnant yet again. Only God knows the number of thoughts that rushed through my mind in just that split second when I found out. Of all those thoughts, not one was to get rid of my baby. I couldn't do that again. There is no way I would reject God's gift a second time.

This time around, the talk I had with God went a little different: *"I lost my friends. I lost myself. I lost a baby. I lost my family. I'm done losing, God. I want to win."*

Once again, I kept my pregnancy a secret. Only a handful of people knew, and they weren't the best people to have in my ear. They tried to give me advice that would hurt me more than help me. For instance, I had one friend at the time tell me I should slip the sonogram of my son under Leah (Jarvis's wife's) front door. Another said I should go take walks in Leah's neighborhood so she could see that I was pregnant. But I wasn't out to hurt her or seek revenge for how she had hurt my friend. Our friendship had ended amicably, as far as I was concerned.

In my eyes, the things those friends suggested were things that someone looking for trouble would do. I didn't have beef with this woman, to be doing degrading things like that to myself, that would in turn harm the friendship I had with Jarvis, in hopes of harming her. Besides, it wasn't my job to tell her. I kept my pregnancy hidden from my mom for about 4 months. When Mothers' Day came, I gave her a card with a sonogram in it and told her that she was going to be a grandmother.

She was happy and sad at the same time. Never in a million years did she expect to meet my baby before meeting the baby's father. I told her about Jarvis with a lot of sugarcoating and withholding of information, but she knew he was married and that hurt her. She didn't see a future with me and a married man. She told me over and over that he would never leave his wife for me. But that's not what I wanted. My Mom didn't understand and I didn't bother to explain.

Jarvis never told his wife about my pregnancy. I never asked him what he thought about the situation. I just knew it wasn't my place to tell Leah I was pregnant by her husband, my best friend. I didn't muster up the courage to tell my dad he would be a grandfather, until I was 8 months pregnant. I didn't know how he would take it. After all, his side of the family is the devout Christian side. I didn't want to be judged for 1) being pregnant outside of marriage and 2) being pregnant by a married man.

Surprisingly, my dad took the news better than anyone. He cried and opened his arms to me. I wished I had told him sooner. Dad made me feel so much better about this milestone that I was about to cross. After I told him, he made me feel like nothing else mattered. He told me, *"Whether you do good or bad people will talk about you, so just live your life and love God."* I went my entire pregnancy without showing. The morning after I told my dad, I blew up like a balloon!

On October 13, 2013 I gave birth to my beautiful healthy son Mathieu *(gift of God)*. Jarvis didn't make it to the hospital for the birth of our son. I wasn't surprised, as I went to all the doctor visits alone too. He wasn't even present for the baby shower. I understood why. Nonetheless, I had a wonderful team with me for Mathieu's arrival: my good friend Sandra (Mathieu's godmother), my little sister Johnna, my parents, my aunt Lude and a friend, Precious who was a part of my support system at the time. My aunt, Arnee was on the phone praying. I was originally only allowed to have two people in the room with me, but the nurse couldn't get over the love in the air. She let everyone stay as I brought life into the world.

At the moment when the doctor placed Mathieu in my arms, nothing else mattered. I thought, *this is me. This is my life. This is all that matters now*. People say having a child changes you and makes you look at life differently. They say it causes you to think before each decision, knowing that every decision that you make will affect that child as well. Mathieu became my world, and I moved back in with my mother. I actually felt a sense of peace, it was technically home.

Jarvis wasn't the type to not be a part of his children's lives. He was a father to Mathieu and still a friend to me. However, the time and effort that I used to put into the friendship decreased as my focus shifted to my son. Soon, that started to put a strain on the friendship with Jarvis, and that's when I knew that we had started to fall for each other. As if we had trauma-bonded, our connection now ran deeper than just mere friends with benefits.

Besides, it had been about a year and a half at this point, that he had been fighting for his marriage. I did not want Jarvis to leave Leah for me. I never felt like he should leave his wife for me. I was rooting for them, but at the same time life was just strolling along for me and I was just and along for the ride. I watched my best friend beat himself up through all that time, for somebody who didn't even care. He never completely put the blame on Leah — he always said it was on both sides — but from the outside looking in, he was in a fight by himself. I was just sitting there watching. Leah knew of all the moves Jarvis and I had made together, but she did not know about Mathieu.

Mathieu was about 6 months old by the time Leah found out about him through social media. By then, I had watched Jarvis get broken down to someone I no longer recognized. I didn't want to lose my friend and I certainly didn't want Mathieu to lose his father. Still, Jarvis was always there when I needed him, even while going through a divorce that I didn't know about until it was finalized.

I watched the father of my son get his life flipped upside down and inside out. He was thrown to the wolves but through it all, he was still a father. He gave no excuses while playing his role, but he was always angry. I could tell he was in a place that he didn't want to be in. The person I had turned into after my grandparents died, is the person I saw Jarvis turning into. I wasn't going to let him navigate this season alone. We were a team. It was us against the world. This next chapter in our lives is what really put us to the test.

The Storm

Chapter 6: Flakka

Here I was, 25 years old, unmarried, with a child, living at home with my mom. It's certainly not what I had pictured my life to be at that age. I wasn't attending school and I was just working and getting by. I had no friends — my world revolved around Mathieu and Jarvis. My mother wasn't having it and was starting to make me uncomfortable on purpose. She couldn't understand how I could love a "nigga" so much.

Me being who I was, I didn't respond to the tough love the way she wanted. I felt attacked, got defensive and used it as an excuse to again avoid her. *Jarvis was still always there for me. Why couldn't she be too?* I was going through life without a clue of how to resolve conflict. I was a good Mom but I felt like I wasn't a good enough person. What did I have to show for myself? I ran to what I knew best —drugs and sex.

My sister, Johnna was 16 at the time and Mathieu was her best friend. She took care of her nephew like he was her own. Their bond was unbreakable. So, it was easy for me to leave Mathieu with Johnna while I ran the streets with Jarvis chasing the next high. This is when a hard drug called *flakka* had hit the streets of South Florida. *Flakka* also known as 'the devil's drug', was a synthetic crystal that could be smoked, snorted or swallowed. Flakka hitting the streets of Broward County was one of the worst drug crises since the crack-cocaine epidemic of the 1980's.

My Mom always told me, *"make your dirt look clean"* and *"nothing in America is free."* I never understood what she meant until I said it to myself out loud one day. She meant that even when you're out there doing bad you should make it look good. So, I decided to make my dirt look clean. In January of 2015 I applied to Keiser University to major in Psychology. I was still getting high and drinking a lot, but I went to school which kept Mom off my back for a while.

Just like I did growing up, I kept up my grades inspired by what I was fighting on the inside. My stepdad was still present, but he didn't say much. If he ever talked about my behavior, it was always to my mom. He never really told me what to do unless I went to him for advice. I wondered what he thought of me while seeing my life at this time.

One night after leaving class, I called Jarvis to see what he was up to and meet up with him. I caught him at a time when he was so high that the look on his face was indescribable. He looked defeated but alive at the same time. He had a blunt rolled as usual, but I didn't think anything of it. He lit the blunt and the smell that came from the blunt was different. I knew it was weed in there but it smelled dirty. One of the first things that I had learned during my early clubbing days, was to never smoke a blunt that I didn't see get rolled.

Jarvis was a druggie, so I knew he had a dirty blunt before. I reached over, took the blunt from him and took a nice hit. That was the night that I tried flakka for the first time, and after feeling that high, it was my mission to smoke flakka from that point on. The flakka gave this euphoric feeling of being free, light, loved — absolutely nothing could compare to that first hit feeling. It was like the molly on steroids. But as time progressed, the more you got high the more you would become like a paranoid zombie during that session.

I had a love-hate relationship with flakka. I loved the escape but hated to get too high, because it's as if I would be locked in my body in one spot and just be stuck high in another dimension until I came back down. Jarvis and I would sit in the car that I had at the time, and smoke from sundown to sunup. You would be correct in calling us addicts at this point. I was still going to work, still going to school and still being a mom, but I had this double life of smoking flakka.

I was able to function when I needed to. It started with me trying to be there for my best friend and father of my child, to me willfully suppressing my own sadness. Flakka took away the feeling that I got when I hated myself for not accomplishing more in life. Flakka took away the feeling I got when I wanted to build a better relationship with my parents but didn't know how. When it came down to dealing with my feelings and cmotions, I would retreat into my shell. It's like everything about mc shut down.

Flakka became the answer to any and everything. Didn't know what to do? Roll a flakka blunt. Off day from work? Smoke a flakka blunt. Bored? Let's get a flakka blunt. The drug was so accessible and so cheap. I worked just enough hours to pay my car note every week, get us drugs and a hotel room to binge. If we didn't have enough money to pay for all three, Jarvis and I would just buy drugs and park the car at an abandoned home and binge in the car.

Tax time came around and that was the worst thing that could have happened. That was the first time that I had so much money in hand at one time. I paid up my car note for about two months, paid my sister for watching my son and got lost in a hotel room with drugs and Jarvis. We did a 9-day binge of no sleep — just blunt after blunt, drink after drink.

Sitting in that hotel room I got so high that I started hearing voices through the walls. I could hear the whores from rooms across the hall getting slapped by their pimps. I heard babies crying through the walls. I heard whispers like they were right next to me. When I closed my eyes, the room started spinning like I was on a merry-go-round. When I opened my eyes, I could see faces coming out of the walls. It's like they were trying to get me but I had a shield of protection over me and they couldn't touch me.

I yelled back at the voices and faces as I paced back in forth in the hotel room. I paced so long I'm surprised I didn't grow blisters on my feet or dig a hole into the floor. I remember clapping my hands over and over like a child trying to focus on one task. But my hands couldn't stop clapping. I always wanted to be naked. I never had the urge to run in the street and roll around, but I did always want to be naked.

We always made sure we were in the car or in a hotel room. When the tax money started running out, we transitioned to walking into abandoned houses. Sometimes we would get lucky and find an abandoned house that still had running water and electricity and crash in that spot. I chased that feeling of being worry-free for so long. Every blunt we rolled, we prayed to God it wouldn't be our last. We prayed to get through another night. We didn't even talk about our problems.

My mother knew something was up — she always knew when something was up. I never understood how she got that feeling until I became a mother. Mom cried out to me to stop. I started being careless and smoking flakka in my car in front of her house. She recognized the difference in smell and knew I was doing more than just weed. She cried out to my dad, but he thought I was smoking weed and told my Mom to just let me be. *The weed won't harm her*, he said. Little did he know, it was more than just marijuana.

My mom cried to me to stop. I wouldn't listen. One day she caught me smoking, and asked me why I was doing that. I responded angrily, *"Why are you acting like you care? There is nothing to talk about, just pretend like it's not happening. Don't talk about it and it will go away. Just leave me alone."*

The look on her face was broken. I gave my mother the worst pain that I could. I kept everything from her except her grandchild. The more I went on the weekly binges, the more she cried. She felt like she had lost me. One night we both stood in the middle of the street screaming at each other, each of us crying out for help in different ways. I never saw my mom break down and call on God the way she did that night. We both cried, but I walked away from her and left her standing in the street. I immediately took another hit to take away that pain.

My addiction got so bad that I would look in the mirror and not recognize myself. I started getting small scabs on my skin and I would pick at them. I was losing weight, but in the eyes of everyone else I looked good. I had always been a plus size girl so people thought I was losing weight on purpose. My world was upside down. I felt unstoppable but weak at the same time. Sex and drugs were the only remedies that made sense to me, so I didn't have to deal with life.

Then, in April of 2016 I find out I was pregnant with my second son, Elias. Once again, I had another purpose in my life. I stopped the drugs during my pregnancy. Me carrying my children was the only thing that kept me from getting high, but the drugs were always within reach. I thought, *if I could let go of my addiction for my child, surely I should be able to let go of my addiction for myself.* But I didn't love me the way I loved my children.

I remember after having Elias, things just weren't the same. My sister was still there for me but she was getting older living her own life. I didn't want to burden her with watching two kids just so I could go back to feeding my addiction. But I took advantage of that opportunity every chance I got.

I saw my life headed towards a dead end. I had dropped out of school yet again and basically survived off of getting high. Jarvis and I had gotten so high that we were acting differently. It's like the high transported us to a state where we became enemies. We fought so much about things that didn't even make sense. We would yell at each other in the middle of the neighborhood at 3am. Jarvis threw bricks at my car in rage. I remember us arguing in the car once, and he got out in the middle of traffic and I drove off and left him while laughing hysterically. It's like something overtook us and we didn't care about hurting other's feelings. I never went out to buy the drug myself, I was always with him. So, when we fought and he left, I was left without the drug and craved getting more of it.

When I realized that I was chasing the high that badly, I broke down and cried out to God. The conversation I had with God under that tree wasn't like any conversation I had with Him before. This was a petition for help. I was in too deep and I finally realized it. I admitted to God that I had a problem and didn't know what to do.

"God, I know you are here. I know You never left my side. I was too caught up in my flesh to even take the time out to make You my main focus. I love you, God. I love my sons. I love my family. Please show me a new way. Give me a new way to make thing right for myself and my children. This is not me! Flakka is what I used to find me in my dark time, and I was supposed to be walking in the light with you, God. I should have been putting my faith in you, God and not the devil's drug. Please, please, please show me a new way. My life is in Your hands. You have all control."

I ended up at the front step of my mom's house and I let myself in. One thing about my mom: she never changed the locks on me. My key always worked. No matter how long I would leave and not call, when I came back to her front door it was always open for me. She never told me I wasn't welcomed. She just always wanted me to do and be better. She fed me that day and left for work. In my heart I knew that even after crying out to God, if the flakka came knocking at my door I would go and take a hit. I turned on the television, and learned that a category 5 hurricane named Irma was making its way through the islands and heading to south Florida. The county was ordered to evacuate to safety ASAP.

In that very moment I knew that this was the way that God had provided for me to find my new path. A lightbulb went off in my head and I called my Aunt Arneè in Indiana. I still don't know what made me call her, but that's who I called. I asked her if the boys, myself and maybe their father could come to Indiana until the hurricane passed. She agreed with no questions asked. Now I just had to find Jarvis and tell him the plan. At this time it had been roughly 2 weeks since we last spoke.

When I finally got in contact with him, I told him that we couldn't keep living like this. I told him that we need to do better for ourselves, in order to do better for the kids. I told him that we have to stop the drugs.

I said, *"I'm leaving for Indiana and you can either stay here or come with me. But either way I'm taking the boys and I'm leaving."*

He said he would come. I packed my kids' clothes and whatever clothes I could find for myself, along with my paintings and packed it into a friend's car because my car had finally gotten repossessed due to missed payments. Jarvis came with a small suitcase of whatever he could pack and we didn't tell a single soul. We left in the middle of the night. Half the state was trying to evacuate at the same time, but we left right before the rush. The drive was 18-20 hours long, but we made it safely to Indianapolis.

Chapter 7: Indiana Beginnings

September 7, 2017 was our first day in Indiana. My aunt lived about 30 minutes away from the city. Indianapolis is definitely different from Florida. The trees look different, the weather feels different, and the diversity that's in South Florida is more pronounced than in Indianapolis. We were welcomed with open arms and smiles by my aunt and cousins. They had prepared a room for us to put our things.

Although I was with family, deep down inside I longed for my own place because when I got to Indiana I was ready for something different. I didn't want to move from couch to couch, or crash in hotels anymore or sleep in the car. At first, my intentions were to go back to Florida with a fresh mindset after a couple of months and get myself on track, but I knew when I got to Indy that I would be there longer than I initially thought.

In November 2017, the kids were adjusting well to the weather, so I decided to find some healthcare for me and them so we could get regular check-ups. That's when I found out that I was 4 months pregnant with Baby Number Three. At this point I boldly asked God, *"What are You doing?!"* As if I didn't play a part in the conception. Finding out I was pregnant put a bit more mental pressure on me and my plans of working and getting on my feet. I went back to my aunt's house from the doctor's visit and just kept repeating to myself, *"What is going on?!"*

That's when I pulled out my Bible and opened it and the first verse I saw was Jeremiah 29:11: *"For I know the plans I have for you," declares the Lord, "plans to prosper you and not to harm you, plans to give you hope and a future."*

That was when I stopped questioning God. My response was *"Alright, I hear You. You got this! We got this."*

While living with my aunt and cousin, I knew time was ticking when I found out words were going back and forth through the family about the move I made, and the choices Jarvis and I had made while we were in Florida. Lots of gossip filled the air, but no one approached me to ask what was really going on. I'm not the type to make gossip be an issue — I let people talk.

Though it was upsetting coming from family, I remembered what my dad always said, *"Whether you are doing good or bad people are going to talk about you. Let them talk, especially if they don't come back to you for the true facts. Love God and pray for them."*

Jarvis, having gotten a job a week into moving to Indy, had gotten himself into a situation at work that caused the police to come to my aunt's house looking for him. That caused some tension in the house for sure. That's when I felt like my cousin was starting to treat us differently. There were more arguments in the house and things went from warm and welcoming to cold and distant. I was in a completely different environment geographically. I didn't even know north from south, or east from west but all I knew was I had to make a decision for me and my family.

I started calling shelters but they were all full to capacity, or didn't accept males. You know by now that I won't abandon Jarvis so I kept seeking a place for us. My uncle gave me a couple of resources that helped people in need with necessities such as daycare and food. We tried to get out of the house as much as we could to not be in the way. It took one especially heated argument where there was name-calling and disrespect between Jarvis and my cousin, for me to draw the line and identify that it was time to go.

Chapter 8: Homeless

On the morning of December 15, 2017, I received a phone call from a man named Mike. Mike said he was the director of a homeless shelter called Family Promise of Greater Indianapolis. I quickly flipped through my notebook to see if I had written the information of that shelter down but I couldn't find the name. Mike told me that there was a spot for a family at his shelter if I was still interested. It was a Friday and he said the center would be closed to the public on the weekend.

He explained that a family that was supposed to enter the shelter had decided on another location. Still a bit confused, I asked him where his shelter was located and if there was transportation. He said he could send a cab and they would pay for it, but that we would have to be ready by 4pm. I had a brief moment with God and in that moment I saw Jeremiah 29:11 again. I accepted the offer and told him we would like to take the spot.

When I broke the news to my aunt, she tried to get me to stay, especially because I was pregnant. She tried to reassure me that I didn't have to make that choice and that I would always be welcomed in her home and loved. She said family gets into arguments and disagreements but the love is still there. I wanted to stay but I just knew that I couldn't. My time there was up. I had to take a leap of faith and trust that God was taking care of me.

As the woman of God my Aunt Arnee is, I knew I would be covered with a shield of protection from her prayers. If anyone were to ever ask me to explain my idea of what a woman of God looks like, I would show them a picture of my Aunt Arnee. We packed up the bits of stuff that we had into a taxi van. Coincidentally, at that moment Jarvis got a call from his grandmother who told him that he has family in Indiana and that he should call them. But me? I was done moving in with family and going from couch to couch. I was tired of being an inconvenience to others.

That's when Jarvis brought it to my attention that he had a warrant in Florida and back pay on child support, saying he didn't think the shelter would accept him. I believed it was an excuse but I wasn't going to argue. Jarvis decided not to go to the shelter, but went to live with his cousin instead. I took the hands of my boys and we got into the taxi and headed to Family Promise.

Tears filled my eyes when I sat in the passenger seat thinking *how, just how did I end up here? Where am I going? What am I going to do with two kids and a pregnant belly? Where did I go wrong? Is this the right decision for us?* I was scared, lost and confused but I put my trust in God.

I remembered Jeremiah 29:11 and held it in my heart: *"For I know the plans I have for you,"* declares the Lord, *"plans to prosper you and not to harm you, plans to give you hope and a future."* (NIV)

The day after Elias turned a year old, I was moving into a shelter. Mathieu was just 4 years old so he didn't really understand what was happening. In his eyes, we were on another adventure, meeting new people and experiencing a different environment. Elias wasn't walking yet so I literally had to carry him and our stuff. when we moved into Family Promise, but within 2 weeks he took his first steps in that shelter. Mike greeted us in the parking lot and paid the cab. We arrived at about 15 minutes after 4pm and I noticed that the families (about 3 groups), were cleaning up and loading into a passenger van.

I was given a brief tour of the center and was then told that we have to get on the van with the other families. Mike explained that the center was only for families to check in and have belongings stored probably in lockers and larger items in the basement. The center also had bathrooms and showers (not all the churches had showers), and two sets of washer and dryer, but every day at 4:30pm we would get on the van to be transported to a church to have dinner and sleep. This explained why Mike said I had to be to the center by 4pm.

At the church, all families had a large duffel bag with pillows and a blanket for each member. That duffel bag stayed at the church even when we went back to the center. But every Sunday we would move to a different church that sheltered us, and that's when the duffle bags were packed up and prepared for the next route. We also had cots for each family member. So, my duffel bag had 3 pillows and 3 large fleece blankets, one for me, one for Mathieu and one for Elias. Because Elias was so young, they provided a pack-n-play for him to sleep in, while Mathieu and I had individual cots. Mike clearly explained all these details to me.

We arrived at the church and were directed to our room with our names on the door. When I opened the door, our duffel bag was already set and cots ready for us. I put my bag pack down and sat on the cot and stared at my boys. They were running around carefree, just being kids, while I cried quietly. I cried, because I felt lost, empty, alone, helpless, pained, confused, angry. I feel like I went through all the stages of grief in the matter of 10 minutes, but the only thing that my body could do was cry. All I could repeat was "God, I'm in a shelter with my kids."

The volunteers at the church walked around and told us that dinner would be ready at 6pm, and that lights out is at 8pm. As you could probably imagine, the food wasn't what I was used to cooking or eating but I made myself content. I was happy that the food was hot. Dinner was green bean casserole, roasted chicken, mashed potatoes and another dish that I left alone because I couldn't tell what it was.

After I made sure my kids were well fed, I started to cry all over again in the cafeteria. The mixed-up emotions from my pregnancy didn't help my life circumstances right at that moment. I was as vulnerable and as stripped down as I could be and I didn't care what onlookers thought. That's how I expressed myself at that moment. At some point while my tears flowed, another mom walked up to me and looked me in the eyes and said, *"It's not over baby,"* in a thick Louisiana accent.

She recognized those tears and knew them all too well. She was with her two boys as well. Deedy was her name and that's the first person who talked to me and actually introduced herself and her kids. She was from New Orleans and had basically done the same thing I did — packed her and her family up in the middle of the night and left. After her twin brother was murdered, she found no reason to stay in New Orleans. She was open with me and cried with me. She hugged me and reassured me that as Moms of little black boys we couldn't give up. We had to keep moving forward and trust that all will work out.

"It's easier said than done but possible," Deedy reassured me. She had been at the shelter long enough to have a job and start saving for a place of her own. She had a good heart, but you could tell life's struggles had given her a hard exterior. I thanked her for her kind words and we went back to our rooms.

The Center hours were from 9am to 4pm, but because one of the families had a daughter who had to be to school early. We had to be to the center by 5:50am in order for her to catch her school bus on time. With that being said, our mornings began as early as 4am, depending on how far the church we were sleeping at was from the center. Waking up that early had to be one of the hardest aspects of the transition for myself and the kids. Not only did we have to wake up at 4am, but we were in the Midwest with the temperature in the negatives, inches of snow and ice on the ground and in the trees. My children and I are from the Sunshine State. We had never seen snow a day in our lives, much less commute from place to place in inches of snow. Those mornings all three of us cried together.

Day 2 at Family Promise was interesting. Mike was in acquaintance with many churches in the area and lots of churches volunteered for different events. This particular day a church was having a birthday party for Jesus. It was around Holiday time so the party was appropriate for the occasion. Mike told the families that if we wanted to attend we could, and that the church bus would come and pick up.

He took me to the side and said I should go and have some fun with the kids. I looked at my boys and said, *"Sure, why not."* When the church bus pulled up, I grabbed Elias in his car seat, told Mathieu to grab his booster and walked outside. I stopped to see the name on the side of the bus and it said *"New Way Community Church, where the spirit of the Lord lives and his people are set free."*

My heart dropped into my stomach. A rush of emotions took over me as goosebumps engulfed my arms and the hairs on the back of my neck stood up. I immediately recalled the conversation I had with God back in Florida when I asked him for a new way. I dropped the car seat to the ground in disbelief as I tried to gather myself. Realizing my pregnant belly through the thick coat I had on, the driver rushed out and helped me load the kids in. All I could say was, *"thank you,"* to the driver and to God.

We arrived at the church and I felt so happy. Just all of a sudden, I felt joy. There was a leaping in my body, but from the outside looking at me you couldn't tell. I didn't even understand where that feeling of joy came from. But I knew that was God hugging me. I walked into New Way holding Elias in my arms and Mathieu walked beside me admiring the Christmas lights and decor. What really got his attention was the music that was playing. Mathieu loved to dance and he was ready to party. My son was way more sociable than I was. So, to him no one is a stranger and anytime is a time to dance and laugh. I loved that innocence about him.

The church welcomed people from everywhere of all different backgrounds. As soon as you stepped foot into New Way you felt a sense of peace — a spirit of love and light. You can immediately tell they served God and his people. Everyone had a smile on their face and offered hugs like you were a biological family member that they hadn't seen in a long time. It was like a family reunion with strangers.

The birthday party for Jesus was for everyone but you could tell the kids were the main guests. They played games, won prizes and ate good food. Mathieu danced and enjoyed himself. Elias was with me watching everyone run around, but he looked happy. In that moment even I was happy.

There was a woman that was directing the choreography and the games that was happening with the youth. She had the biggest smile on her face as she danced around with the kids and clapped as she passed around the mic. There was a light surrounding her, a light that shined so bright that you couldn't help but to be in good spirits when around her. Mathieu clung to her instantly. I noticed because he kept dancing around her.

Being the protective mother I am, I told him to calm down a little and she looked at me and said, *"Honey, he's okay, he's dancing for Jesus."*

And with that she grabbed Elias from my arms and danced with him too. As my kids danced and played at Jesus's birthday party I got a chance to breathe. A rare opportunity to just sit and breathe. It was only day 2 and for the first time I wasn't crying tears of guilt and pain. I shed a tear of joy because my kids were happy. They were safe and they were able to be kids.

After the kids ate enough cake and won enough prizes, they all received goody bags and we headed back to the church bus to be dropped off at the center. The Woman With The Bright Light walked up to me and gave me a little flyer with the church's name and the volunteer work they do for the community. The church had clothes drive, canned food drives, a daycare and so much more. The part that stood out to me was church service on Sunday.

I thanked her for the flyer and told her, *"I'll see you tomorrow if I find a ride."* In my head I thought, *I'll walk if I have to.*

She pointed at the bottom of the flyer and it said, *"Contact Theresa about transportation."* The woman smiled and said she was Theresa. *"Call me and I'll make sure you have transportation. We have a church van and the shelter isn't far."*

I made sure to call Theresa that evening and make arrangements to get picked up for church service the next morning. The kids and I didn't have much clothes. We got dressed in sweatpants, sweatshirts and beanies to stay warm. Theresa kept her word and made sure we had transportation to make it to church on time. When we arrived I noticed a big banner on the lawn. It was a picture of Pastor Brown and First Lady Theresa Brown. I just smiled.

During church service, I smiled because Theresa, the Woman With The Bright Light was the pastor's wife who also ran Youth and Sunday school. She was also a member of Women of Virtue, a group that provided a space where the women of the church could fellowship with each other. Little did I know, Theresa would be an important figure in this new phase of my life.

The ride back to the center was a bit like reality setting back in. Around everyone I kept my composure, but I was melting on the inside. *How long am I going to be doing this? Will I have my baby in a shelter? How am I going to take care of a newborn moving around like this?* Then I remembered service and the topic was 'Giving your child back to God!' There was God hugging me again. A shelter is the last place any person would want to call home, but that's what it was for me and my kids. We had someplace safe to sleep and hot food in our bellies. Still, I cried every single night for about 3 weeks straight.

Christmas came and my aunt showered us with gifts that she had been secretly wrapping since the day we moved up. I found a ride and we picked up the gifts and brought them back to the shelter. The church that we were at also gave out stockings, gift cards and gifts for all the kids and parents. My favorite gift was 3 blankets: my name was embroidered on a pink one, Mathieu's on a red one and Elias's on a green one. It felt like we actually had something of our own.

After one of my favorite uncles, Chris, passed away Christmas morning of '99, my mom was never in the Christmas spirit. So, to celebrate with my kids was different and fun despite the circumstances. The hardest part for me was ringing in the new year in a shelter. I always believed that however you start the year is how the year will go. So, in my perspective, entering the new year in a shelter meant being in a shelter for the year, and I wasn't happy about it at all.

It was time to commute to another church, and it was there that I met Ericka. She was the mother of a new family that had moved into Family Promise. She had two boys and a girl, and had just moved to Indiana from Ohio. Ericka caught me crying in my room and just like Deedy, hugged me and told me, *"It's going to be alright."* She sat down and talked with me for a while. We got to know each other and basically became really good friends. We made sure we woke up on time in the mornings. We would watch our kids play with each other while we talked about living a better life.

Ericka made it easier to get through the days. I'm not sure she knew that. She would come up with the most random conversations with me and we were okay with it. We made each other laugh and eased our troubles by having conversations about our favorite soaps, perfumes and makeup. Ericka loved make up. She and Deedy were definitely a breath of fresh air. I knew I would have them around as friends even after we progressed out of the shelter.

Attending New Way Church service became a regular routine for me. I was getting closer to God without even realizing it. I made the choice to get baptized on January 14, 2018. It almost didn't happen, because the pool was still too cold because it was snowing outside. Theresa caught me in the parking lot and said we would have to reschedule the baptism to a time when the water was warmer.

I politely declined. *"I'm getting baptized today. My aunt is on her way to watch this glorious event and I'm not going to let anything get in the way. Sister Theresa I'm getting baptized today."*

All she could do was say, *"Alrighty, then let's go. I love the spirit! Won't he do it!"*

We laughed in unison. The water was indeed cold, but the fire burning inside me to be a better me, overpowered it. When I came up out of the water I felt free, liberated and on top of the world. The night before I got baptized was the last night I cried at the shelter.

At the church we went to that night to sleep, the volunteers had gift bags for the family. In my bag was my all-time favorite body wash. No one at that church knew that that was my favorite soap. The bags were donated randomly to the families. I stood there and cried while the volunteer stared in confusion. I told her how I was tired of the donated hotel soap that we got in our bags and to be gifted with body wash, let alone it being my favorite, felt like I was being hugged by God. No one understood that moment but me and God. It was a nice baptism gift from God, and it reassured me that I wasn't alone on this walk.

God is real.

As time progressed, so did my growing belly. I didn't want to know the sex of my baby. I just wanted to continue my pregnancy and be surprised. Jarvis had 7 boys and no girls, so my best guess was that I was having another boy. The time came for me to find a job and get started on stability, but that was hard because no one wanted to hire a woman who was 7 months pregnant, let alone one who lived in a shelter. In the eyes of a stranger, I looked irresponsible. I was a woman with no man beside her, hauling two children and a belly. I continued to apply to random jobs with no luck.

One night after being in the hospital with my sons all day because of a stomach flu, Mike, the director picked me up in his personal vehicle. It was after center hours, so he came to drop us off at the designated church. As he was driving, he looked over at me and asked me what my plans were with the newborn and being in the shelter. I didn't have an answer. I just expressed that I was taking it one day at a time and that God will make a way.

Mike then continued to tell me about another pregnant woman who was at his shelter that had transitioned to another shelter that housed pregnant women and children. It was a maternity home for homeless women, named the O'Connor House. The home was in Carmel, Indiana — the safest city in America with a crime rate of less than 1%. It was about 35-40 minutes away from Family Promise. Mike said he would call the home and see if there were spots available if I was interested. My main thought was, *will I have to commute back and forth like we are now? If so, I might as well stay where I'm at.* But I took what Mike said into consideration and spent the night Googling The O'Connor House.

The O'Connor House's website was filled with pictures and various information such as their mission and purpose. The next morning I told Mike that I would think about it some more. He went ahead and called the home for me, but gave me the number and said I should call as well.

To even be a candidate for a home tour, I had to go through 2 interviews — one over the phone, and the second in person. If I passed the interviews and agreed to the rules, terms and conditions, I would get a tour and a welcome home.

It took me 10 days to pray and talk to God, to decide whether I was ready to go to yet to another place and start over. I found out that that's where we would also be sleeping, so I wouldn't have a daily commute to a church. I also learned that the program was 18 months long, and that I would have time to have my baby and then get a job. Hearing this, I couldn't decline. After having my phone interview, I had a follow-up in person interview. This interview took place at a Chik-fil-A, where I met with the director, Susan and one of the house managers, Jesse. Both interviews went well and I was accepted to be part of the program.

When looking at the criteria to be in the program, I literally met every requirement by the skin of my teeth. Mathieu was at the cut off age. Aside from being pregnant, I could only have 2 other children with me, and no drugs or weapons were allowed. But the main rule is I had to be pregnant. If I didn't see the signs in front of me and know that God had a plan for me, I probably wouldn't have accepted the offer.

Although we were in a shelter, Jarvis was literally 5 minutes away. If I moved to The O'Connor House we would be close to an hour away, and the church I just got attached to would now be 45 minutes away. I would be taking yet another leap of faith but I believed it was something I had to do. It felt right. Jarvis understood the steps I had to make. Even so, he didn't join in that journey with me and I wasn't asking him if I could go. I was telling him that the kids and I were going to Carmel.

I called Theresa and told her about the transition. She said if I still wanted to attend service she will make a way for me to be picked up, and once again she kept her word. The church driver drove to Carmel every Sunday morning and picked me up by 8am so I could get to the church service on time. Mr. Vernell, the church bus driver, and I became good friends because of those Sundays bus rides. His wife was always with him in the front passenger seat. I loved hearing them talk about their own children and grandchildren. The interaction they had with each other always had me laughing Sunday morning before church.

Chapter 9: Moving Day

On January 26, 2018 Mike helped me pack all my belongings into his van as I said my farewell to Ericka and Deedy. Mike drove me all the way to Carmel. I can't even remember what we talked about. I was so nervous about the move. I kept wondering about how Mathieu would adjust, *How would I adjust? Are the women there crazy or are they nice? Is it pretty on the outside but a totally different story on the inside? There were so many* emotions and thoughts and scenarios playing in my head on the ride to The O'Connor House, but when we pulled up all I could say was, *"thank you, God."*

I let out a breath of relief as I took in the view. The home was a big house with 8 bedrooms housing 1 Mom each, a nice spacious kitchen, a bathroom with 3 showers and 3-bathroom stalls like you were in a fancy gym shower room. There was also a basement fully equipped with the necessities for kids to play and an extended basement that held donations such as clothes, shoes, diapers, hygiene care et cetera, for the moms and children. There was an office for the therapy sessions and a manager's office with a bedroom in the back for when the house managers spent the night.

There was a chapel, and a huge backyard with a playground. I could hear Mathieu in the back seat becoming excited about the playground in the backyard. Just when I thought the house couldn't get any bigger, there was an attic that could be an entire house where I came from. It was literally a house with everything we needed to be comfortable. I felt so blessed to be a part of the program, and I had 18 months to get it right. My due date was in March, so the house managers reassured me that I had time to just rest. The word *rest* felt like a weight was lifted off of my shoulders.

Rest meant I could settle and nest while I waited for my baby. *Rest* meant I could finally think. *Rest* meant I could finally not worry. *Rest* meant not having to walk to the bus stop in the snow with my kids to head to a museum just to get out of the center for the day. *Rest* meant not risking my safety, slipping and falling on ice outside trying to load children onto a van while being 7 months pregnant. *Rest* meant I could breathe again.

I walked up the stairs and all the bedrooms had names of women of the Bible on them, and my room was the Lydia room. I walked in with Mathieu and Elias and saw a pack-n-play already set up and a stackable bunk bed. Mathieu was on the top and I got the bottom bunk. It was a small room but I made it big enough for us. It was my room and that mattered. I was content with it because I didn't have to wake up at 4am. Eventually as Moms progressed out of the house I got to switch to a bigger room. I was the only Mom that would have three kids living in house after birthing.

In my room was also a welcome gift basket made out of a laundry basket that came in handy in our stay. The basket contained a towel, shampoo, conditioner, feminine products, toothpaste, toothbrushes, a notebook, a Bible, a planner and many other much appreciated necessities. There was also a random card in the basket with Jeremiah 29:11. When I saw it all I could do was smile and accept another hug from God, because at this point I was beyond convinced. I knew I was highly favored by the Most High. I didn't see fully what those plans were, but my steps were ordered and I received it with open arms.

At TOCH you couldn't just lie around and do nothing all day. Something had to be done, even if you didn't have a job yet. 'Something' meant watching parenting videos, or Financial Literacy videos, but filling up your schedule with a to do list. You could start writing goals down and steps to reach them. The day had to be productive, all while keeping your child by your side unless they were taking a nap, in daycare or school. I knew there was a method to the madness of the structure, so while many moms complained, I saw the bigger picture. Besides I didn't want my kids out of my sight in a home full of strangers.

TOCH was making me do what I would have to do when I progressed out of there into the real world. It was preparing me to become responsible and accountable at the same time. During the day I called all the health care numbers and changed my address. I made sure all the necessary paperwork that had to be filled out for child care and health care were turned in. I got my driver's license from the state of Indiana. I worked on completing my checklists every day and realized that little by little, everything was falling into place.

All the moms had chores that we rotated every two weeks. The house had volunteers that took us to doctor appointments, work, school and any productive errand we had to run. Before you get a job, the basic needs were met, such as clothes for Mom and necessities for the baby. These included diapers, wipes, baby blankets, socks and hair bows. All were provided by donations that were dropped off to help the moms in the house. Never in a million years did I think there was an opportunity like this. The love from volunteers, staff and donors showed me that this world still has a chance.

The group of Moms that I got to house with were brave, quiet, strong, loud and definitely resilient. Our children were bold, smart, carefree and they adapted to our situation better than we did as Moms. For some reason, everyone accepted me with ease. I always listened to what everyone had to say and gave them advice on making the right decision for themselves. God was ALWAYS thrown in there to remind them that they were loved and reassure them that they got this thing called life under control as long as He was put first.

I found myself giving the moms in the house a different perspective on how to view the experience. Of course, I had my weak moments but for the most part God had already showed me that I was going to be fine. So, I enjoyed my stay at TOCH. I didn't look at it like a jail, like most of the moms in the house. I saw TOCH as an opportunity to do better. It was a new way out, to be free. I learned a lot about myself in the mandatory therapy sessions we had every week. I was happy. I was reaching goals and setting more. I felt strong. I felt I had a purpose and I was worthy — worthy of the plans God has for me.

TOCH also assigned me a mentor whose name was Lindy. Lindy baked cookies that melted in my mouth and made my heart smile. I could never just have 1 of her cookies. She was an amazing person, inside and out. She listened to me and didn't judge me. She was my perfect match. Lindy was battling with breast cancer but you couldn't even tell by her glowing spirit. She reminded me of my Aunt Arnee who had also beat breast cancer and was walking the path God intended for her.

Lindy was also a volunteer for the house, so when I needed rides, I would often ride with her. I really enjoyed those car rides. She listened to me and wasn't afraid to share her life experiences with me as well. I called her at 3am once so she took me to the hospital just to be in false labor. We laugh at that night every chance we got. She welcomed me like the daughter she never had. I can honestly say that ours was a very special bond.

March came and went. My Aunt Arnee blessed me with a baby shower but I was still pregnant. Anxious and days past my due date, my doctor finally agreed to induce me. I was having unbearable contractions and gave into getting an epidural. Well, the epidural was inserted too high into my spine and caused a blockage from my neck down to my toes. I couldn't feel anything. I tried to remain calm but it became hard to breathe. The doctor tried to reassure me that everything was fine and that I was breathing, but I went into a panic attack. I passed out 3 times in the hospital.

The last time I came to, I had papers shoved in my face to give permission to vacuum my baby out. I found the courage to muster up the words, *"NO, THANK YOU!"* Loudly I said, *"If it's time, I'm ready to push, but you will not vacuum my baby out."* Vaguely accepting my decline, the doctor had a look on his face like they knew they messed up. Before I could blink, there were about 10 nurses and doctors in my delivery room. Still numb from the medication, I have no idea where the strength came from, but we all know God is always working. I took a deep breath and I birthed my baby into the world with three strong pushes.

My Aunt was with me the entire time, praying and talking to God the way she knows best. The doctor placed the baby in my arms and didn't even announce if it was a girl or boy. Eager to know the sex I raised my baby up in the air and cried out, *"It's a giiiiiiirrrrl! Oh my God! It's a girl!"* Lindy and Jarvis were also present for the momentous occasion. Although they walked in 5 seconds after I successfully pushed Azariah out, Jarvis cut the umbilical cord. I gave birth to my baby girl Azariah *(with God's help)* on April 2, 2018 — an experience I will never forget. The best part was knowing I had somewhere safe to bring her after we left the hospital.

Going back to The O'Connor House after giving birth to Azariah was a different experience for me. First of all, I now had a daughter. For the previous four years of motherhood I had raised boys and now I had a daughter! I enjoyed every second of it. By the beginning of May, I had started aspiring to major goals and wrote out steps to achieve them. My ultimate goal was moving out! I planned to stay the entire 18 months but God knew what I needed.

As I was getting the ball rolling on my checklist, in July 2018 I got a call from my sister. It was 3 days after my birthday. My Mom had gotten a stroke while at the hospital for other reasons. I was devastated that I couldn't just hop on a plane and go home to her. As the firstborn child, I was supposed to be taking care of my mother, but I was thousands of miles away and couldn't get to her.

All I could do was call my prayer partner, Theresa and ask her to pray with me while I tried to breathe. Theresa and I hadn't kept up with being prayer partners the way we should have, but whenever we needed that prayer we didn't hesitate to call. Theresa prayed for me and my mom while I sat and petitioned God to hold my mother together.

Theresa prayed a beautiful prayer on a phone call with my mom. Her prayer gave us hope that Mom would be OK. If Sister Theresa didn't hold a special place in my heart before, she definitely had my whole heart now. Because I was so helpless in that situation, I saw in my mind's eye myself going backwards. I saw myself not reaching my goals. I saw myself letting go and not caring again but I didn't want that!

My Mom having a stroke was just a distraction from the plans God had ahead of me. If I had canceled all my goals and broke the rule by leaving the house without letting TOCH know, I would fail again. The more scared I got about Mom's health, the more God showed me that He had her in His hands. My sister, my brother and my stepdad were there for support, and I was only a phone call away. I couldn't just leave where I was. I believed that God was taking care of this. I just had to stay on track. I'm glad my mom understood, even when others judged me for not going to Florida. I tried though, and the more I tried, the more my plans to leave failed. I took it as God telling me to stay put.

Through the process of praying with Mom over the phone, we got closer. The relationship wasn't perfect, but it was building. Our conversations had more "I love you" and fewer "leave me alone". That's when I realized part of my growth was having to experience forgiving my mom, as well as forgiving myself. The more conversations I had with her, the more I came to know that the molestation I endured affected her more deeply and painfully than I had thought.

It was embarrassing to her, and made her feel like a bad mother. She was angry and lost just as much as I was then. She was supposed to protect me and she felt like she failed. At a young age, I couldn't understand that that's how she felt, because we didn't express ourselves well or communicate directly in the home. So, at an early age I was taught to keep my problems to myself and also run from them. I utilized the chapel in TOCH more than I thought I would. I read many scriptures and said many prayers.

New
WAY

Chapter 10: God Does All Things Well

Things were falling into place. I was approved for childcare vouchers. Mathieu was going to Head Start. Elias and Azariah were also going to daycare so I had time to go to school and look for a job. In June 2018, I got accepted into Ivy Tech Community College to study Human Services. My hope was to become a social worker and help homeless women and children out of hardship situations. Either that, or hopefully get a chance to speak to women, mothers and teenage girls and encourage them that life doesn't end when they run out of options.

I ended up landing a job at the same Chick-fil-A I had done the TOCH intake in, in August 2018 and I absolutely loved it. I was able to work and save so much money that I was able to move into my own place. I was given the award "Woman of Spiritual Strength" by my mentor and TOCH staff at one of the Appreciation Awards that the house held for us accomplishing our goals. Lindy also gifted me with one of her cancer awareness bracelets and the scripture on it was Jeremiah 29:11. She told me that it was her favorite scripture that got her through her struggles. As I felt God hug me yet again, I hugged Lindy. It gave me goosebumps the way God spoke to me, and reassured me.

Despite the ups and downs I endured while at The O'Connor House, I knew it was part of my purpose. I kept my faith through it all. There were days where I wanted to pack my things and walk out of the house. *But where would I go? And how would that be serving my purpose?* Furthermore, the ups were more than downs. By the end of November 2018, Jarvis and I had a talk and both of us were at a point in our lives where we were ready to take yet another leap of faith and make our move together as a family.

Mathieu had turned 5 on October 2018 and reached the cut off age at the house. Of course, since I moved in before then we were welcomed to stay and finish the program. However, I had surpassed the goals I set and it was time to make my move and bless another mom with my spot. The amount of money that we saved individually was combined and we found ourselves a place to stay with our kids. We paid first and last security as well as 2 additional months of rent, to keep us afloat as we continued to work.

I walked out of The O'Connor House and into my own spacious 2 bedroom, 1 bath home on December 15, 2018. It was exactly a year from when I had walked into the shelter at Family Promise. I managed to reach every single goal I set and was gifted a car from TOCH through their car program. The promise I made to myself not to spend another Christmas or New Year's in the shelter with my kids was kept. The best part was I lived 5 minutes away from New Way Church and the annual birthday party for Jesus was coming up. The kids and I attended the party, this time as church members. It was an amazing feeling.

My coworkers at Chick-fil-A got news of my accomplishments and blessed my family and I with furniture, Christmas gifts, bikes for the boys, towels, blankets and beds. You name it and they blessed us with it. I was overwhelmed with gratitude. TOCH also blessed us with cleaning supplies and more gifts for Jarvis and myself as well as the kids. While unpacking, I came across the notebook that TOCH had put in my welcome basket. I had used the notebook to write down my prayers. Every single prayer written in that notebook had become a reality.

From moving out of the shelter into my own place, to Jarvis staying out of trouble, to his child support warrant being lifted, to him getting a chance to see and spend time with his 3 boys from his previous marriage. God delivered, and was still delivering! I hugged God back with prayers of gratitude. I made it our mission to wake up on Sundays and go to church. Living closer to church and having my own transportation made it easier for me to be more involved in church activities. That's when I started to notice the change in Sister Theresa's energy levels. Sister Theresa was battling cancer.

Sister Theresa passed away January 5, 2019 from bile duct cancer. Her passing broke my heart into pieces. The role she played in my journey was indescribable. She drove all the way TOCH to bring me interview clothes when I was applying for jobs. She gave me the best words of advice as an older woman and as a friend. Every Sunday she would hold Elias or Azariah because they would be loud in church, and it gave me time to listen to the Word.

Not only did she have the best words of encouragement, but Sister Theresa was encouraging in the flesh. The love she had for God and serving others couldn't be matched. The sheer number of lives she touched reminded me of my grandfather. She will forever be missed. It was hard explaining her passing to Mathieu, but weirdly he said he understood.

God has not only carried me through my hard times, but He carried Jarvis as well. The growth I saw in him while we overcame life's trials was remarkable. While I was at TOCH, Jarvis was at his cousin's house preparing himself to be the man and father he felt he should be. He proposed to me in the summer of 2020 on my birthday. I gave birth to our second daughter, Nyla Elyse *(winner of God's promise)* in August of 2020 in the middle of a global pandemic.

I still stay connected with some of the moms I met at TOCH, but most of all I stayed connected with TOCH. I hosted Bible study with new Moms in the house, and volunteered to give speeches at events to help raise awareness of the help and resources being provided around the community.

Trusting in God through my trials taught me to focus on the steps in front of me and not the entire staircase. Focus day at a time, one goal at a time and before you know it, you're at the top. You are always one decision away from an entirely different life. Sometimes our lives have to be completely shaken up to help us realize and be re-directed to exactly where we need to be. Don't be afraid to take that leap of faith because when you land you will be unstoppable. Remember that the plans that God has for you are definitely to prosper you.

I can now look in the mirror and be happy with what I see. I'm still growing and learning more about myself, but my faith in God will never waver again.

I never told my mom about uncle Ed. Honestly, I don't even want to burden her with those thoughts. I still haven't expressed my childhood pains to my father either. I am examining the traumas and facing them on my own through therapy. It's my job to forgive and heal through these wounds because they molded me into the woman I am. I realized that not facing those demons head on would continuously put a toll on the relationships I have with friends and family.

I wasn't hiding my true feelings behind the drugs anymore, but I wasn't facing them either. Inadvertently, I was harming the new life that I was building. God placed me in the right spot at the right time to understand why I went through my trials. I'm using what I learned and experienced to help others in ways I didn't know I could. I have joined in my grandmother's mission and am now Director of Social Work for the La Paix Foundation. God is definitely not through with me yet.

There is peace in
a new way.

And the peace is
the new way.

www.ingramcontent.com/pod-product-compliance
Lightning Source LLC
Chambersburg PA
CBHW051548120626
46551CB00013B/1425